I0901907

FEATHERED FRIENDS

PIGEONS

Madison Parker

NORWOOD HOUSE PRESS

Library of Congress Cataloging-in-Publication Data:

Names: Parker, Madison.
Title: Pigeons / Madison Parker.
Description: Buffalo, NY : Norwood House Press, 2025. | Series: Feathered friends | Includes glossary and index.
Identifiers: ISBN 9781684502837 (pbk.) | ISBN 9781684502844 (library bound) | ISBN 9781684502851 (ebook)
Subjects: LCSH: Pigeons--Juvenile literature.
Classification: LCC QL696.C63 P375 2025 | DDC 598.6'5--dc23

Published in 2025 by
Norwood House Press
2544 Clinton Street
Buffalo, NY 14224

Copyright © 2025 Norwood House Press
Designer: Ocean Books
Editor: Kim Thompson

Photo credits: Cover, p. 1 Snehaaa Patel/Shutterstock.com; p. 5 gergosz/Shutterstock.com; p. 6 Snehaacua Patel/Shutterstock.com; p. 7 Attractive Photographer_1/Shutterstock.com; p. 8 Douglas Jennifer/Shutterstock.com; p. 9 Milkovasa/Shutterstock.com; pp. 11, 17 stockphotomania/Shutterstock.com; p. 12 Micha B/Shutterstock.com; p. 13 Bruno M Photographie/Shutterstock.com; p. 14 Sergey lavrishchev/Shutterstock.com; p. 16 YIUCHEUNG/Shutterstock.com; p. 19 FotoBuy24/Shutterstock.com; p. 21 battybattrick/Shutterstock.com

All rights reserved. No part of this book may be reproduced in any form without permission in writing from the publisher, except by a reviewer.

Printed in the United States of America

Some of the images in this book illustrate individuals who are models. The depictions do not imply actual situations or events.

CPSIA compliance information: Batch #CW25NHP: For further information contact Norwood House Press at 1-800-237-9932.

Find us on

TABLE OF CONTENTS

What Do Pigeons Look Like?

Pigeons are our feathered friends. These birds have round bodies and short necks. They have small heads and short **beaks**.

A pigeon's feathers are usually gray. Pigeons have shiny green and purple areas around their necks.

They have red or orange eyes.
Their feet are red or pink.

Where Do Pigeons Live?

Pigeons live in cities and towns all around the world. They like places where there are lots of people.

Pigeons make nests on building **ledges** and under bridges. They use twigs and bits of trash to build them.

How Do Pigeons Grow Up?

Pigeon eggs are small and white. Baby pigeons, called squabs, **hatch** in about 18 days. Squabs grow into adult pigeons in just four to six weeks.

What Do Pigeons Eat?

Pigeons like to eat seeds and **grains**. They often find food on the ground in parks and on city streets.

They also eat food that people drop. Pigeons are not shy about eating near humans.

Pigeons **peck** at their food quickly. They can eat a lot at once. Pigeons use their beaks to pick up food from the ground. They visit bird feeders for a quick snack, too.

What Sounds Do Pigeons Make?

Pigeons **coo** softly when they are calm and happy. The sound is gentle and soothing.

They make a louder cooing noise to call other pigeons. This is a deep sound.

Pigeons hiss when they feel **threatened**. This is how they tell others to stay away.

Pigeons clap their wings when they take off to fly. The action makes a sharp, snapping sound.

What Funny Things Can Pigeons Do?

Pigeons **bob** their heads when they walk. They spin in circles when they are happy. Sometimes, they puff up their feathers and look like big round balls.

GLOSSARY

beaks (beeks): horny, pointed jaws on birds; bird bills

bob (bahb): to keep moving up and down quickly

coo (koo): to make low, soft, murmuring sounds

grains (graynz): small, hard seeds, especially the seeds of wheat, corn, rye, oats, rice, or millet

hatch (hach): to break out of an egg to be born

ledges (LE-jiz): flat places on buildings or cliffs; surfaces that stick out like shelves

peck (pek): to strike something or pick something up with the beak

threatened (THRE-tuhnd): in danger of being harmed

THINKING QUESTIONS

1. What does a pigeon look like?
2. What is special about the sounds a pigeon makes?
3. How does a pigeon show it is smart?
4. What do pigeons eat?
5. Why do you think a pigeon is a feathered friend?

INDEX

ABOUT THE AUTHOR

Madison Parker spent her childhood in the city of Chicago, Illinois. A farm girl at heart, today she lives in Wisconsin with her husband and four children on a small farm with cows, goats, chickens, and two miniature horses named Harley and David. Her favorite dessert is vanilla frozen custard with rainbow sprinkles, even in the winter.